C000141892

Worry Box

Managing anxiety in young children

by
Dr Hannah Mortimer

Acknowledgement
With acknowledgement to Scholastic Ltd for permission to adapt activities (pages 33, 34 and 38).

A QEd Publication

Published in 2007

© Hannah Mortimer

ISBN 978 1 898873 49 5

British Library Cataloguing
A catalogue record for this book is available from the British Library.

Published by QEd Publications, 39 Weeping Cross, Stafford ST17 0DG
Tel: 01785 620364
Fax: 01785 607797
Web site: www.qed.uk.com
Email: orders@qed.uk.com

Printed by Read Me Printing House, Poland.

Contents

Introduction

Who the book is for

This book is part of a series written to help adults provide emotional support to young children aged 4 to 11. Sometimes aspects of their social and emotional development which are underdeveloped get in the way of their happiness or well-being and need working on. This book focuses on managing anxiety and the next in the series looks at anger management (*Fireworks: managing anger in young children*). The books are written in an accessible and practical style so that a parent, carer, support assistant, childminder or mentor can work out the most suitable approach for the individual child concerned and 'pick and mix' activities and talking points.

Why was this book written?

In the author's experience, there are several very useful books available for supporting older primary and secondary age children in groups (some of these are listed on page 43) but fewer are available for individual children aged 4 to 11. The author found herself adapting material to suit these younger children and also writing individual packages so that parents or professionals could support the children they were working with. The children themselves came with a variety of needs:

- Some had been referred to a child psychologist or behaviour support teacher because of a recognised difficulty in emotional and social development – a very short 'fuse', a high level of anxiety or poor social skills.

- A few parents or carers recognised that their child was being significantly affected by a major change in their life (such as a bereavement or a family breakdown) and were asking for advice on what they could do to support their child and minimise any negative emotional effects.

- In some cases, teachers and parents had identified a child as having additional or different needs on account of a social and emotional difficulty and a piece of work had been identified at a special educational needs (SEN) review meeting, such as 'anger management' or 'stress counselling'.

- In other cases, parents simply saw that their child's short temper, anxiety or inability to make friends were acting as barriers to their child's happiness or well-being. They wanted a discreet and family-centred approach for helping their child to cope better.

We know from research on supporting individuals after major traumas that the best people to help and support them are usually those nearest and dearest. Only if we become 'stuck' in dealing with our grief, anxiety or anger do we need more specialist help. In the same way, the author found that when she gave families 'a job to do' in order to tackle their child's

4

emotional difficulties, families usually found the work they did together helpful and supportive and family relationships grew closer in the process. Without a practical framework it is difficulty to 'get started' and a book such as this can act as a starting point for more open communication and more sharing of feelings within the family.

Of course, if you try this approach and the child is just as anxious at the end of the course, you should not hesitate in seeking further professional support. You should also stop the course and seek advice if it is making the child more anxious than before. If the child has been following the approach at school, then a referral from the SEN co-ordinator to a behaviour support teacher might be an option. If you are working together at home, then you might ask your GP to consider a referral to the Child and Adult Mental Health Services (CAMHS).

'Talk through' approaches

The books use a 'talk through' approach to provide a framework for the adult and child to talk together and work together. You might have met this approach before in the book *Taking Part* (Mortimer, 2000) which allows adults to talk through the statutory assessment of SEN with a child. These frameworks should not be followed verbatim and should be used flexibly so that each piece of work seems to flow naturally and feel appropriate to your situation. You are encouraged to think creatively as you work together with the child and to adapt or even design your own sessions as they develop. Though written as an interaction between an adult and child, it is up to the adult to phrase the wording and adapt it to suit the situation.

What do we know about emotions?

We know that anxiety is chemically based and controlled by a complex and finely balanced system within the brain and the nervous system. We know that it forms part of an important mechanism for affecting our behaviour and originates in the 'fight or flight' mechanism we needed for survival as cave dwellers. It was important for us to have a rapid mechanism that allowed us to see a beast and make split second decisions to either chase and attack it or to flee for our lives. It was no good pausing to think about it. This is why the emotional part of our brain is sometimes called the 'primitive' area of the brain – it acts without logical thought and almost despite ourselves.

We may have evolved and developed much higher thinking skills, but our emotional brains continue to be vitally important for learning which things in life to avoid and which to approach and explore. Very young children are inevitably driven more by their emotional brains than their logic – they are all 'needs and reactions'. However, in time, toddlers and pre-school children develop the language and understanding to link their emotional feelings to their words and their experiences and thereby to develop 'emotional literacy'.

The fact is that our emotional brains can switch in without us being fully aware of why or where the feelings are coming from. Some people talk about this phenomenon as forming part of our 'emotional intelligence' – if we can understand where our feelings are coming from and what emotional experiences or 'baggage' have formed them, then we are emotionally intelligent individuals. For many of us, the picture is more complex and we have work to do on developing our 'emotional literacy' if we are to be better able to handle our emotions.

That, in a nutshell, is what this series is about – helping even young children to develop their emotional intelligence when it seems that their emotional brains continue to shout louder than their logical brains. Some children find it hard to integrate their emotions with their experiences and they remain very emotional individuals who react rather than consider.

To support these children, the adults in their lives may need to find out where the strong feelings are coming from and do what can be done in order to address the root causes. Sometimes this will involve family work on relationships within the family, addressing any history of abuse and emotional damage, any deep-seated phobias and any ongoing fears and stresses. This book does not cover that work. At another level, the child can be helped to deal with the emotional reactions that occur, understand where the feelings are coming from, challenge some of the thinking it seems to rouse in them and thereby learn to control their reactions. These books address those areas.

The book is based loosely on cognitive behaviour therapy in which the child is helped to think about their feelings in a different way and thereby to feel more in control of them. You will also find some of the ideas from an approach called 'solution focused therapy'. These approaches are not magic wands and should never be used as a sticking plaster for serious emotional problems – 'fixing' a behaviour on the surface cannot also address an underlying emotional difficulty. That is why the approach is sometimes used as part of a wider menu of support with the aid of an outside professional. Nevertheless, if an emotional behaviour is getting in the way of a child's progress and happiness and if the child recognises this and wants to do some work on it, then it is well worthwhile trying the approach in this book within a home or educational setting.

The benefits of relaxation

Relaxation techniques are valuable for helping children cope with anxiety and stress and this is why this approach includes a session on 'relaxation'. It can be difficult to help very young children to relax and the easiest way is to keep your own voice and attitude calm, relaxing and reassuring. Slow breathing helps children control muscle tension and anxiety, and a useful approach is to teach children how to breathe slowly with you. A typical slow breath would be for you to breathe in for a slow count of 7 and out for 11.

'Visualisation' has also been used to help children to relax and this is also included in one of the sessions. Children can be helped to clear their minds and imagine a warm, relaxing and safe place to go to. They can picture this in their minds and retreat to it when they need to feel secure and relaxed.

How to use this book

Chapter One helps you to get started. You need to think about who will do the work and how to involve and engage the child fully in what you are doing. Chapter Two suggests twelve sessions that can be used flexibly and adapted to suit your situation, whether working at home with your own child or in an educational or out-of-school setting. There are also useful activities suggested for working on relaxation with any child. At the end of the book is a resources section with helpful books and other resources. Throughout the book you will find activity sheets and questionnaires to enlarge and photocopy or give you ideas for drawing your own versions. These are for the child to complete with your help and to stick into their work file or scrapbook. There are also some comments from adults who have used or adapted the approach with children they have worked with.

Chapter 1

Getting started

Involve the child

First of all you need to identify that there is a problem. There is no point embarking on this work if the child sees no need or does not understand what it is about. Something brought you to the point where you obtained this book and considered doing some work with the child. Put this into words and write it down. For example: 'Sam is such a worrier. He is finding it harder and harder to get out of the house in the morning and go to school. Sometimes he cannot eat and gets a tummy ache. He worries non-stop about his homework. I just want him to be happier about school.'

So far, you have *your* reasons for working together but they might not be Sam's. Look at what you have written and you might find one or two statements that are concrete, indisputable and clearly a problem for Sam. For example: 'You are getting horrible tummy aches. They stop you eating and you need food like a car needs petrol in its tank. Shall we try to stop them happening?' or 'You are getting into trouble for not getting all your homework done but I know it is because it worries you a lot. When your Worry Box shouts too loudly it stops you thinking straight. Shall we do some work on this together?'

By now, you might also realise that there are other ways in which you can address the problem by looking at the underlying cause. If he is this worried about school or about homework, then you must arrange a meeting with the teacher and talk about it. In other words, your plan of action now has two levels – working on the underlying cause and managing the emotional reaction to it.

Who is the best person to help?

If you are following the approach at home and there are two of you, talk to the child about who they would like to do their work with. Do not be upset of your child chooses the other parent – usually each parent is good for meeting different needs in their child. Whichever of you is chosen, make this an absolute priority and keep regular, protected time for it. Make sure you also have enough time to clear your own mind and become calm and receptive before you begin.

If the approach is being used in school or another setting, then decide who will be regularly available for the child and who the child already feels close to and can trust. This might be a personal support assistant or a teacher who has been released by a classroom support assistant. Some schools might have carefully selected and screened volunteer mentors or parent helpers. This kind of work is also possible to do in out-of-school settings where there is a small amount of training and ongoing support from, for example, a Sure Start team. Family support workers might be well placed for this work and these kind of approaches are also used by community nurses or occupational therapists in Child and Adult Mental Health Services (CAMHS).

A shopping list

You will need:

- an A4 box file, preferably new, 'cool' and one the child has chosen;
- a pack of brand new felt-tip pens in many colours;
- a craft box with scissors, glue stick, hole punch, thicker felt-tips etc.;
- a scrap book, A4 file pad or stack of A4 paper.

Put everything in the box file and keep it safe and out of circulation between sessions.

A quiet corner

You also need to decide on a quiet place to be together for about 45 minutes each time for about ten to twelve sessions. Because the whole course will take several sessions, it is best to find a slot in your week when you both know you can be together on your own – plan it rather like a music lesson. You might decide to work on the child's Worry Box once a week. You might enjoy it so much that you choose twice a week. Do not rush it any faster than that because it needs time to 'cook' in the child's head between sessions!

Planning your sessions

Read the whole book first so that you know broadly what you will be doing together. Plan the first two or three sessions carefully, but then let the course take its own direction as your work together proceeds. Keep the content of future sessions secret from the child so that each session comes as a good surprise. Explain to the child that a lot of the work you will do is for fun, but it also has its serious side. By the end of the worry course, you will both have learned lots about how the child's Worry Box works and how it can be kept under control ready for when it is really needed.

Ages and stages

Though the text tells the child to 'read' or 'write' something, you should adapt how you do the activities depending on the age and stage of the child. Younger children will need you to do all the reading and writing but even four year-olds can tell you what they want you to write for them or may want to copy pieces into their scrapbook if you help. Do not feel that you have to finish each session at one sitting. Once again, stay flexible and allow each to run into the next as you find some take longer or less time than others. Above all, 'go with the child' so that you are both really engaging with and thinking about your work together.

I wanted to use this approach because my eleven year-old was getting so anxious about tests such as SATS and felt so badly about failing things. Actually, it was quite out of character because he has always been one of the strongest academically in his class. But his nerves just got the better of him and he could not write a thing on one of the papers. After the results, he felt really bad about himself, as if he had let us all down. It really shook his confidence and he was quite low for a while. We wanted to help him see that he was not stupid – it was simply his nervousness that got in the way of thinking clearly. The course gave him more confidence to feel that it would not happen again next time he has to sit an important test.

Mother of Harry, aged 11

Chapter 2

Twelve practical sessions

These sessions are written as an interaction between an adult and child. This avoids specifying gender and also makes the text seem more personal and directly relevant. For very young children, you will need to do all the reading of course. For all children, you need to interpret the text flexibly and alter the style to suit your situation. The words simply give you both a starting point for the work you are doing together.

The sessions are numbered but should not be followed blindly. After the first three sessions, adjust and develop as the child and the situation begin to lead you. The very first session is deliberately more impersonal than the rest to give you both time to settle in.

If you are working as a professional, make it clear that your work is normally confidential. You will agree with the child what can be shared with other adults in their life and what cannot. The only times when you would need to break confidentiality is if you have concerns about the child's safety or about breaking the law. Child protection procedures are paramount over everything else you do in this course.

Below are some comments made by a parent of a six year-old about using this approach.

I used the approach with Jamie because his behaviour has been really difficult since my partner and I had an acrimonious break-up two years ago. His teacher felt that he was not being naughty but that his confidence and self-esteem were really low. The educational psychologist became involved and told me that he was really quite anxious about things. It was as if Jamie was grieving. Jamie needed to talk about my partner and what had happened but felt that it would upset me. He seemed to be blaming himself for what had happened. So we did work on two fronts – we used a life story book* and also helped him work on his anxiety which was causing him to feel insecure and to act up. I didn't want to take him to a clinic – I wanted to keep it all within the family and the psychologist helped us do this using this approach. We adapted the sessions a lot by seeing which Jamie seemed to respond to best.

Parent of Jamie, aged 6

*A life story book is just that – a scrapbook put together by an adult and child describing the child's life, family members, homes and major events or life changes. Photographs and the child's drawings are used to illustrate the story. The life story book then becomes a useful prop for fetching out and talking about whenever child or carer need an excuse to talk about personal events and feelings.

Session 1	Making a work box

Hello . . . . . Well done – you have decided to do some work on your anxiety to try to help you stay calmer, feel better and help you think more clearly. We will call your anxiety your 'Worry Box'. Some of us have worry boxes that shout louder than others and make us feel that bad things are going to happen most of the time. I hope you really enjoy what we're going to do together and that it is useful. Take a moment to ask me any questions or share any worries you have about our work together now if you like.

Your first job is to prepare your work box. This is, in fact, your new box file. Decorate a large label and stick it onto the front – it should say 'WORK BOX – STRICTLY SECRET' and have your name on in large decorated letters. You won't need me for all of this session, but we'll make sure we can be together alone some of the time so that you can share it with me and I can admire it.

Well done . . . . . that's the end of your first session! Give the work box to me so I can keep it somewhere safe.

Notes for adults

Keep this work personal by using the child's name frequently. Try to let the child work as independently as possible on their work box so that they feel proud of what they have done and personally involved with the work you will be doing together. Use this session to settle in together and keep it relaxed and encouraging.

Session 2	All about me

Welcome back. In this session you are going to be finding out about *you* and what makes you tick. We are all different and that is why some of us are good at one thing, some of us at another; some of us worry a lot, some of us do not.

Talk to me about your family. Write down all the things each member of the family is good at. Which are the same? Which are different? Write down who is a worrier – I think you will find we all are! What are the different things you each worry about, do you think?

Here is an example of what the lists might look like.

What we're all good at	
Mum	Cooking supper, reading stories, fixing the computer, doing hair, making me feel better, playing badminton, singing in the bath, making people laugh
Gran	Going on trips, mending things, telling stories, making the dog do tricks, giving presents, telling brother off
Brother	Lego, playing commandos with, shouting, telling scary stories
Me	Drawing pictures, singing in the bath, playing cricket, swimming, reading, making people laugh

Who worries in our family?	
Mum worries	when I argue with my brother; when she has to pay big bills; when she gets sent for by the teacher; when the car won't work; when Gran is ill
Gran worries	about Mum worrying; about Uncle George who had that trouble
My brother worries	about nothing I can think of, though he gets cross when I go into his room
I worry	about not getting things right; about not seeing my Dad; about tests at school; about Mum

Draw a picture for your Worry Box on two sheets of paper. The first should show your head (looking happy) with a huge think bubble at the top. Into this space write down all the things you are good at and feel proud of. I will help. On the next page, draw yourself looking worried and write down in the bubble space all the things you worry about. There is an example here to look at. It's OK to tell me – it won't worry me because I'm here to help you learn all about your Worry Box! We'll talk together about what will be confidential – what are 'good secrets'?

Actually, we all have *two* kinds of brain inside our heads. We each have a **logical** brain that is good at thinking, remembering, learning things. Write down a list of things your logical brain has learned to do. Here is what it might look like.

My logical brain has learned to . . .	
✔	read a book
✔	write a short story
✔	argue with my brother
✔	remember things . . . like what I did last birthday
✔	how to use my Playstation
✔	how to talk and understand things
✔	how to do calculations

We also each have an **emotional** brain that is good at feelings, worrying and telling our logical brain whether things are safe or not. You probably know that human beings as we know them today developed from cave dwellers thousands of years ago. We had to have these two kinds of brain – one that was good at reacting quickly and one that was good at thinking – you had to know whether to run for it if you saw a beast or whether to chase the beast and eat it up! Let's think about that for a moment. Our emotional brain is our 'Worry Box'.

So far we have learned that we each have a Worry Box and it is an important thing to have. If we did not have a Worry Box we would all fall asleep. Some people have very quiet Worry Boxes. They never get worked up about anything. They are called 'laid back'. But at the same time, they might not get really excited about anything either so life could be a bit boring.

Other people have very noisy Worry Boxes. The trouble is, their Worry Box is shouting too loud for their logical brains to think clearly. Think about times when this has happened to you and talk to me about them. Sadly, when our Worry Boxes get too noisy it can cause problems for us. Let's write down some of the times when your Worry Box shouts too loudly. What happens next? Here is an example.

I really get worried when . . .	
☹	I have to get up in the morning to go to school – my tummy aches and I can't remember things
☹	when the teacher says we are going to have a test – my head goes blank
☹	when I hear shouting and arguing – I just want to cry

But we now know that we can train our Worry Boxes to shut up a little – and that is exactly what you are going to do. So you will end up noticing your Worry Box, but then telling it to stop being so silly and to let you get on. That's the aim of our work together. Is that OK with you?

Let's gather all the writing we have done this session and put it in your work box. Would you like to file it in the big file or shall we mount it with glue in a scrapbook? You choose.

That's it for today!

<table>
<tr><td>**Session 3**</td><td># My emotional brain (Worry Box)</td></tr>
</table>

OK, so we now know a little more about what makes you tick. Today we are going to draw a mind map all about your Worry Box.

A mind map is when you get a huge piece of paper and felt-tips and do lots of branches and connections as more and more thoughts occur to you. Draw a mind map with you in the middle and use a mixture of drawings, words, arrows and links to describe yourself – who you are, what you like to do, what kind of a person you are. Use lots of different colours. I will help you with ideas, but I won't tell you what to put – you decide. Here is an example.

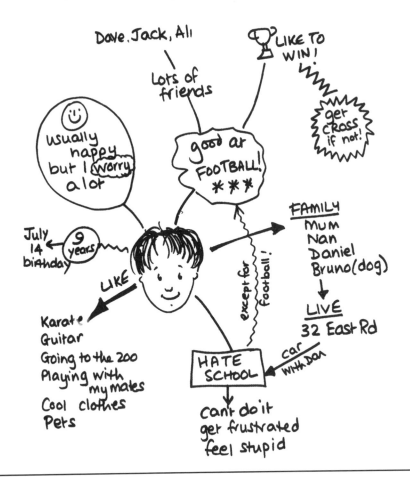

Now let's start to think about your emotional brain or Worry Box. Work with me as you complete the questionnaire on how things are going for you. It's OK to share things with me – I won't worry and we have already talked together about what is secret.

How are things?
What are you really pleased with at the moment?
Why do you think this is going so well?
What's not going so well for you?
Why do you think this is?
What do you think would help you?

Now think very seriously about a 'miracle question' and write the answers as you and I talk about them together. Imagine that you wake up tomorrow and all your troubles and worries have gone – someone has been able to wave a magic wand over you in your sleep and there has been a miracle! Think through your day. What is the first thing you would notice – how do you know that things have changed? Then what would you notice next? Think of all the things that would be very different from now.

If I woke up tomorrow and all my problems and worries were gone – this is what I would notice... First .... then.... then...

For example: 'I wake up. I notice that I feel really happy because I've got lots of friends and I'm looking forward to seeing them this afternoon. I've got lots to do – we play football together and they come back to my house to play on the computer. I'd feel happy and busy and the fluttery feeling in my tummy would be gone – all because I had lots of friends.' Now hang onto that good feeling. Over the next few sessions, let's work out together how to help you work your own magic.

Session 4   Stress

Hello again. When your Worry Box starts to shout, it has an effect on your body called 'stress'. The thing which makes it start to grumble or shout is sometimes called a 'stressor' but we'll call it a 'trigger' – something that 'starts you off'. In your case, think about what your big triggers are – what starts your Worry Box off? Here is an example.

	What starts me off . . .
☹	Someone calling me names
☹	Thinking I can't do something
☹	Worrying about Dad
☹	When Mum shouts at me

There is *good* stress and *bad* stress – if we didn't feel stress we might not get up in the morning. Stress makes us do things – like running, getting up, learning things, like saying 'hello', like remembering our lunchbox and so on. When stress actually leads to us doing something useful, it works well for us. Think of some examples – here are a few to get you started:

	Good stress . . .
✔	Feeling excited about a party and getting ready for it
✔	Waiting to open presents on your birthday
✔	Getting ready for a football match

But sometimes stress gets bottled up and can't go anywhere. That's when it becomes *bad* stress. Let's spend a little time seeing whether you have bad stress that needs dealing with.

Work though the next questionnaire with me and decide how you are affected. I could do it too, perhaps, so that we are sharing it together. Let's find out about what happens to you when you worry – when your Worry Box starts to shout, what does it make you do?

What happens when you worry? N = Never S = Sometimes O = Often A = Always	N	S	O	A
1. I worry about everything				
2. I can't concentrate				
3. It makes me feel sick				
4. It gives me a tummy ache				
5. I can't get to sleep at night				
6. I wake up really early				
7. I feel all jittery inside				
8. I get headaches				
9. I think I'm stupid and no good				
10. I can't relax and enjoy myself				
11. I want to hide away				
12. It goes round and round in my head				
13. I eat too much				
14. I don't feel hungry at all				
15. I blame myself for everything				

If you have any of these problems, then they are well worth working on, aren't they? This is why we are working hard together to find out more about how your Worry Box works.

Spotting a trigger

If you are going to learn how to handle your Worry Box, you need to be able to spot those things around you that are likely to cause you stress – we called these 'triggers'. This is important because we are all different. Some people's greatest trigger might be going to a party where they don't know any of the people because they are shy. Other people find that tests and exams set them worrying. For others it might be something to do with their families, with going to school, with changes in routine or with getting things wrong.

Let's look together at this story about Victoria and see if you can spot the triggers.

Victoria is nine. She has just moved to a new school and she finds it hard. Her previous school was rather strict and old-fashioned and she always had to stand up when she talked to a teacher. The trouble is, she can't seem to stop herself doing this and the children at her new school are making fun of her. She wants to be friends, but they seem to have decided that she is 'sucking up' to the teachers and they don't talk to her. Now they have started to call her names and she can tell that they are talking about her behind her back. She can't tell the teachers as she feels that would make things worse. She is worried about telling her mum who split up from her dad and is still very upset about things. Recently Victoria has started to feel sick in the mornings and has not wanted to go to school.

What is stressing Victoria?	The reactions of other children.
What effect does it have on Victoria?	It makes her feel ill and worry.
What are the triggers?	At first, name calling and talking about her, but now it has become going to school.
What could Victoria do about it?	Find a way of talking to someone – try to make friends one at a time with the other children – learn not to stand up when she talks to a teacher – find interests to share with the children in her class – stay calm and not react – develop a plan so she feels more in control.

Now let's pick out a couple of role plays which would be most helpful for us both to do. Each one is about a child called 'Mo' – you can imagine Mo to be a boy or a girl and whatever age you decide. You choose. We will spend a little time role playing these together and for each one we will think about:

- the biggest trigger;
- the effect it has on Mo;
- what would be a bad thing to do to reduce the stress;
- what would be a better thing to do to reduce the stress;
- and plan our advice for Mo.

Role play

Someone at school keeps calling Mo names – it makes Mo want to miss school.
Every time the teacher sets a test, Mo feels jittery and can't think straight.
Mo can't concentrate because of thinking about Mum and Dad.
Mo can't get to sleep at night because of nasty emails being sent.
Mo has been invited to a party, but has nothing cool to wear.
Mo thinks that the maths teacher is picking on him/her.
Mo can't stop thinking about Mum's hospital appointment.
Mo is the only one in the class not to have a mobile phone.
Mo's dad has lost his job and Mo worries all the time and can't concentrate.
Mo can't do maths and the teacher is very strict.
Mo's friends keep falling out and asking Mo to take sides.

Invent more to suit you and your Worry Box.

Now think about the triggers in your life. We all have different ways of reacting to anxiety and stress that kick in at different levels. The picture on the next page shows you an example of this for a ten year-old called Dan. The curve is all to do with how many demands are being made on you – that means how many things you are being expected to do and how awake and ready to go you are. Have you noticed that when you feel really worried about something it makes you more 'aroused' – perhaps you start pacing up and down or bite your fingernails, perhaps your heart starts to beat faster and perhaps you breathe faster? We all need to be a little bit aroused to think and learn best – the part at which we do best is just before the top of the curve.

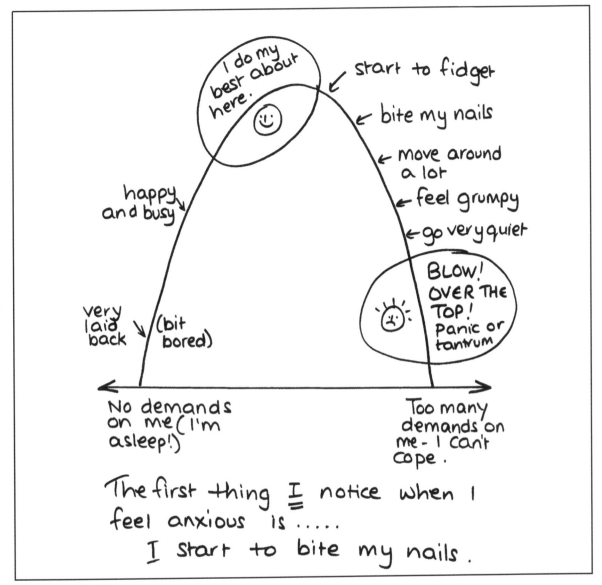

My stress by Dan

Now you try to make a similar diagram for you, marking on the curve what you begin to feel or think as you become more aroused or anxious. What is the first thing you notice as you begin to feel anxious? Then what happens? Then what? What you have drawn is a very special diagram and a very useful one. If you can spot what you feel at different stages, you can actually learn ways of making the symptoms go away and this makes you feel less anxious – you can control where you are on the curve so that you are at the right level for *you*.

Session 6	Getting support

Our Worry Boxes tend to be quieter when we have lots of support. You have your family, your home and also your friends. If you can learn what things support you, you can actually plan extra support when it come to worrying times. So let's have a talk about 'friends' and write down your thoughts on the sheet.

Friends What do you think a really good friend should be like?	
What would they do for you that was friendly?	
What would you do together?	
What would you talk about?	
What would your friend be like?	

This will help you to draw your own list of friends and helpers on the next sheet. In the middle heart put all the people who will support you whatever (like your family and close friends) – in the outer heart add the others who are also there for you (like teachers, other friends, doctor, etc).

Others who help me

My nearest and dearest

Me

The rest of this session is for drawing your own friends and family and we will write a little about each of them for your work box. How does each one help to make you happy or stop you worrying? What worries would you talk to Mum/Dad/Nan about? What worries would you talk to your friends about? What worries would you talk to your teacher about?

Good luck! Make sure all your work sheets, pictures and pieces of writing are safely in your work box – it must be getting quite full now!

| Session 7 | **Being healthy** |

Worry Boxes are also much quieter if you stay healthy and fit. Have you have noticed that things get more on top of you when you're not well? Have you noticed how you can worry more, for example, when it is the end of term, when you are very tired, when you haven't eaten properly or when you are fighting a cold? Let's draw or do some writing together to explain how your health affects your Worry Box – and how your worrying affects your health.

Here are some ways in which people try to stay healthy. Let's talk about these together and decide which we feel is the most important for you, what is going right at the moment and what we need to try and improve for you.

Staying healthy

- Eating lots of fresh food, fruit and vegetables.
- Having good friends.
- Having fun with other people.
- Doing sport and exercise.
- Enjoying hobbies.
- Not eating too much junk food.
- Keeping happy.
- Getting enough sleep.
- Eating a proper breakfast.
- Not eating too many sweets.
- Being the right weight for your height.
- Taking time to relax.

Now let's talk about these and draw up a list like the one on the next page for your work box.

Things for staying healthy	
The kind of food I usually eat in a typical day.	
The friends I see regularly and have fun with.	
The sports and exercise I do regularly.	
My hobbies.	
What makes me happiest.	
When I go to bed; when I wake up and how long I sleep.	
My weight and my height.	

Now we'll look at the information we have collected. Do we think there is anything we need to work on here? If we find that there is, we'll draw up a target and spend the next fortnight seeing if we can begin to change things for you. Let's think of a suitable reward for you if you stick to your plan. If we can improve your health, we have a chance of keeping your Worry Box quieter.

My health target

Start date: _____   **Target date:** _____

This is what I will do:

This is who will help me and what they will do:

This is what will happen if I stick to my target over this time:

Session 8	Speaking out

Do you remember we talked about 'bad stress' – stress that couldn't go anywhere because it didn't lead to action? We said this was like bottling things up. Sometimes we are not very good about saying what we feel and we may need to do some work on being 'assertive'. Talk to me about what this means. Should you always say what is on your mind? When is it best to 'bottle it up'? For example, if your grandma gave you a present and you didn't like it, would you tell her? Let's think of some more examples.

If they are feeling stressed, some people speak out – this is being assertive. Some are passive and just let other people 'walk all over them' or just 'switch off'. Others get angry and 'stroppy'. Have you noticed this in people? Try thinking of some examples.

Puppet play – being assertive

We'll find some puppets or some of your toys to act out a few situations and show what a difference it makes. Here is an example you could try with two puppets, Gib and Gub.

Take two puppets. Gib snatches Gub's favourite toy.
First, try making Gub say and do nothing – what does Gib do?
Now have Gub kick up an enormous fuss and lash out. What happens then?
Now have Gub say, 'Please don't take my toy. I'm playing with it. When I've finished, you can have a turn'.
You can also try having Gub ask for help from an adult.

Let's talk about each situation.

Here are some ways in which people learn to be more calm and assertive. See if any apply to you:

• Listening carefully to other people and respecting their feelings.
• Not raising your voice in an angry way.
• Telling people how you are feeling.
• Asking nicely and calmly for things.
• Trying to work out how other people are feeling.

- Saying sorry when you know you've done something wrong.
- Not expecting people to tell you how good you are all the time because you know it yourself.

Sometimes people are too aggressive and this gets them into trouble. Does this apply to you ever?

- Shouting at people.
- Demanding things.
- Being rude and swearing at people when you don't get your way.
- Making others feel sad or uncomfortable.
- Hurting other people's feelings.
- Hitting out or kicking other people when they don't agree or want to play.

If we feel that there is an area to work on here, then we can plan another target and reward for you – we can use the target sheet on page 27 again if it will help.

You are now ready to think about your own style of dealing with stress and to make plans for changing if you find that this would be helpful. You have thought of a few ways of doing this already:

- It could mean being more assertive when this seems right.
- It could mean spotting the triggers and finding a new way of dealing with them.
- It could mean that you ask for more help when you feel worried.
- It could mean working harder on staying fit and healthy.
- It could also be that you need to relax more and that is what we are going to look at in the next session.

Notes for adults – activity 'I'm OK!'

Here is an additional activity you can include for a child who lacks confidence.

What you need
A mirror.

What to do
This activity is helpful if a child is particularly worried about something they feel they cannot do and if this is clearly unrealistic. For these children, the 'little voice' inside them that tells them they are no good can actually get in the way of them improving. You need to combine the approach with practical help. For example, if it is spelling tests they are worried about, help them with their spelling as well as helping them tell themselves they are getting better at it.

Sit together in front of the mirror and think of a little voice that you can put in place of the one that seems to tell the child that he or she is no good. For example, here are some that other children invented:

I can do it if I try
Every day I'm getting better at spelling
It's not my fault spelling is hard – with help I'll get better at it (e.g. for dyslexia)
I'm a friendly person
I'm worth knowing
I am just as important as everyone else
I have a right to be happy
I'M COOL

Make a joke of this at first and try saying it in different voices and tones until you find ones that really sound as if you mean it. Now use it as a mantra to repeat with meaning every day or whenever life is worrying.

Session 9	**Think peaceful thoughts**

Welcome back! Are you sitting comfortably? Then we'll begin!

Here is an imagination game. Look at 'My special place' on the next page and write your own very special version. We can photocopy this onto a larger sheet of paper for you or draw our own photograph frame for you to write or draw in. If you want to, you can do some writing about your special place in the picture frame and then do a separate painting or drawing on a much larger piece of paper. Spend most of this session thinking about and creating your own special place in your imagination. When you feel really happy thinking about your special place, tug your ear down.

Keep your special place safe in your work box to look at again. When you start to feel your Worry Box grumbling, try closing your eyes for a moment, taking some deep slow breaths and seeing this special place in your mind's eye. Tug your ear again and the picture should come back. Practise now – think of something really worrying. Hold it for a while – now relax and go to your special place!

Let me show you how to take your pulse. I will place my fingers lightly against the dimpl e just behind your wrist on the thumb side, or I might feel the side of your neck. You have to do this gently and lightly so that you do not stop the blood pumping around the body. You can actually learn to calm a fast (stressed) pulse by breathing and imagining – magic! And as your pulse goes down, so your Worry Box becomes quieter and your logical brain can think clearly again. Let's try this.

You need to practise going to this special place at least three times through this next week and learn how to do it.

My Special Place

My special place looks like this

When I am there, this is how I feel

Here is an additional activity you can include to teach visualisation.

What you need

A script for a simple visualisation exercise. Try adapting the idea below or have a look at some helpful scripts suggested by Jenny Moseley in *More Quality Circle Time* in order to encourage relaxation (see page 43).

What to do

Encourage the child to lie back comfortably on cushions. If you are working with your own child at home then bedtime is an ideal time and place for this activity. Suggest that you rest and relax for a few moments. What does it mean to 'relax'? Talk about how it means keeping still and keeping peaceful. Talk together about places they love to be in when they want to be peaceful. Some children might suggest the seaside, a garden or a favourite room. Suggest to the child (but do not insist) that he or she closes eyes and takes some deep, slow breathes with you. Count slowly '1, 2, 3' as you breathe in and '1, 2, 3, 4, 5' as you breathe out more slowly. Now read your 'visualisation' script to the child. Here is an example:

Imagine that you are in a beautiful room. There are long curtains and a thick carpet. Feel the carpet between your toes as you wiggle them. On the floor are some beautiful cushions. You lie down on the cushions and stretch out. Can you stretch out your legs? Point your toes out, now relax and make your legs go still and floppy. Can you stretch out your arms? Now let them flop back onto the cushions. Take a great big yawn. Now you relax. Imagine your own special room and look around it, admiring all your favourite things. Feel the happiness pouring through you as you rest.

After some more 'imaginings' and slow breaths (as long as it is not bedtime of course) help the child liven up again gradually.

Now it is time for us to (have drinks/finish our work together/go out) so we are going to open our eyes, have one more big stretch and get up slowly. Wasn't that relaxing!

This activity has been adapted from *Special needs in the early years: medical difficulties* by Mortimer (2002) published by Scholastic .

Here is an additional activity you can include to teach relaxation.

What you need
Somewhere with cushions and rug to relax.

What to do
Make yourself familiar with the rhyme below. When a child needs to relax, encourage them to lie back and make themselves comfortable. As you say the second line, help the child tighten each foot then let it relax and fall back gently. For the second line, tighten knees and then relax. Gradually work up from toes to eyes, tightening and then relaxing each part of the body. Take the verse very slowly so that, at the end of the verse, the child should feel relaxed all over.

Here comes peace!
Here we go! It's reached my toe . . .
Oh me! It's reached my knee . . .
Oh my! It's reached my thigh . . .
That's funny! It's reached my tummy . . .
Have a rest! It's reached my chest . . .
Staying calm, it's reached my arm . . .
Go to bed, it's reached my head . . .
Close my eyes, pretend to sleep . . .
PEACE . . . PEACE . . .

When you have finished relaxing, start moving again slowly and gently, rising slowly to your feet and stretching. In time, children can learn the relaxation routine if you chant the words slowly. They can also learn to begin to relax when you reassure them and softly say, 'PEACE'. As you learn the rhyme, talk about how each part of the body feels when it is tight and then when it is relaxed.

This activity has been adapted from *Special needs in the early years: medical difficulties* by Mortimer (2002) and published by Scholastic.

We need a recorder and tape or a recordable CD to make our own relaxation tape. Let's work out together how we will do this – perhaps I could read the script into the recorder as you do the actions so that we get the timing right. We will spend the whole of this session getting this organised and practising using it. We will finish by drawing up a relaxation timetable for you for the next week, writing down when and where you will practise relaxation. For the first three weeks, this should be every day. Then it should be just two or three times a week or at worrying times.

Notes for adults

Find a quiet, warm and comfortable place to do your relaxation where you will not be disturbed. For professionals working with children out of home, this can be adjusted for lying back in an armchair with hands placed loosely in the lap rather than having to lie down. Most children also enjoy relaxing music playing quietly in the background as you record your script. Speak slowly and steadily, leaving gaps where you need to – this is why it is helpful for the child to model the actions as you record the text. Slow the whole pace of the actions right down. Do not rush anything.

Just relax! Lie down flat on your back, close your eyes and take a minute to go as floppy and soft as you can. Imagine you are a big cushion settling down onto the carpet. Let your feet fall gently outward. Let your arms lie by your sides with the hand slightly upwards. Try to breathe slowly and steadily, letting your breath become smoother as it flows in and out like soft waves on the shore.

Now you are feeling floppy and calm. Tighten your feet, pushing the toes backwards towards your head – hold it – and now let go. Let them fall back into place. Feel the difference as you tighten once more – then let go.

Now tighten up your knees so that your legs stick out like sticks. Hold it for a few seconds. Now let go. Can you feel your legs going floppy? Do this once more – tighten – then let go.

Now squeeze your bottom and the tops of your legs together and hold this. As you breathe out, let them relax and become floppy again. Do this once more – squeeze – hold – and relax.

Tighten your tummy and hold it for a few seconds – then relax. Take a few slow breaths. Now tighten, hold, relax and breathe once more.

Spend a few minutes just noticing how floppy and soft the bottom half of your body has become. Think of each part and check that it feels completely floppy and soft – your toes – your feet – your heels – your calves – your knees – your thighs – your bottom – your tummy.

Clench your fists tightly and feel the difference as you let go and help your hands become floppy again. Try this once more – clench tight – now relax.

Stiffen your elbows so that your arms poke out like sticks. Hold this – and relax again. Notice the difference. One more time – stiffen – hold – relax.

Tighten your shoulders and hunch them up to your neck. Hold them tight and then let them flop. Take a breath. Now tighten once more – hold – relax and breathe. Let the whole of your arms go completely soft.

Close your eyes very tight and notice how this feels. Let them relax again and try this one more time – squeeze shut – hold – and then relax.

Frown so that your forehead becomes tight – hold it – and now let your face relax and go smooth. Frown once more – hold – and relax. Notice how it feels when your face is smooth and relaxed and there are no frown lines.

Clamp your teeth shut and close your lips tightly. Feel how tight this feels – and now relax. Try this one more time – tight – now loose again.

Lift your head for a moment – feel how heavy it is and let it fall gently back to the floor. Lift once more – hold – and gently back. Turn it to the right until it feels just a little tight – then to the left – and now let it lie back gently into position. Turn to the left, then over to the right – and now back into place.

Now think about your breathing. Feel the air flowing smoothly in – and out – and try to think only of your breaths coming and going like the gentlest of waves. Spend a few minutes staying as relaxed, soft and floppy as you can.

Now it is time to bring your body back into action. Waggle your toes – your legs – your hands – your arms – shrug your body – and gently rock your head – and very soon it is time to get up.

After we have counted, move slowly and carefully as you get up again so that your head gets used to being up in the air again – 5 – 4 – 3 – 2 – 1 and – very slowly – up you get. Well done.

Notes for adults – activity to support relaxation – balloon therapy

Here is an additional activity you can include to teach a breathing technique.

What you need
A bag of party balloons.

What to do
Play with the party balloons, blowing them up and letting a few whizz uncontrolled around the room as the air escapes rapidly. Now invite the child to watch you carefully. Start to blow the balloon up and share their anxiety as it becomes just that bit too tight. What might happen? (It might burst). What do we need to do? (Let some air out). What would happen if you knocked my hand now? (Try it and see – the balloon whizzes out of control).

Explain that when your Worry Box is too busy, it's a little like being a balloon that's just too tight – the slightest knock sends you spinning into a whirl. What do you do when you get knocked? (Burst into tears/lose my temper/feel panicky).

Practise blowing the balloon up and then letting air out gently. Explain that when you are feeling tight, you can breathe slowly and gently and your balloon won't feel so tight. Practise breathing slowly and gently – slightly longer out than in. This might lead on to trying some of the breathing games that follow.

Notes for adults – activity to support relaxation

Here is an additional activity you can include to teach slow breathing.

What you need
Make yourself familiar with the rhyme below.

What to do
This activity is to help a child breathe fully and deeply. Perhaps they are calming down after physical exercise or becoming too excited. First help the child place their hands lightly on their lower chests so that they can feel their chests move, pushing their hands outward and upwards, as they breathe in and out. Ask them to copy you as you show them how to breathe calmly. It will take a little time, so continue your own regular pattern of breaths until the child matches yours. Now chant this rhyme softly as you breathe slowly in for the first line and out for the second. Emphasise the numbers in the rhyme and say the words more softly. In time, you can replace the rhyme with a slow count of 'one – two' using a slow count as the child breathes in, and a count of 'three – four – five – six – seven' (for a slightly longer breath out).

One little alligator, two little alligators,
Three, four, five, six, seven little alligators,
Resting in the river where nobody goes,
Waiting for the moment when they see your toes!
One little alligator, two little alligators,
Three, four, five, six, seven little alligators,
Snoozing in the river in the midday sun,
Best not wake them anyone!

Hannah Mortimer

This activity has been adapted from *Special needs in the early years: medical difficulties* by Mortimer (2002) and published by Scholastic.

Session 11 — Getting organised

Another way of quieting your Worry Box is to plan ahead and be really well organised. Is this you? Practise choosing priorities by using the next sheet. Enter 'A' if this is something you always have to do (in other words, it is a 'priority'), 'S' if it is important that you do this sometimes and '?' for 'only if there's time' if you fit this in between everything else.

What should my priorities be? A = Always S = Sometimes ? = Only if there's time	A	S	?
1. Watch TV			
2. Eat meals			
3. Do my homework			
4. Play outside			
5. Tidy my room			
6. Go to school			
7. Chat on the web			
8. Text a friend			
9. Go shopping			
10. Take a shower			
11. Play on my computer/playstation			
12. Chat to my family			
13. Get ready for school the next day			
14. Listen to music			
15. Read a book/magazine			

Now look at each of these again. Perhaps you have entered that you need to do something 'sometimes', like chatting to your family. Let's talk together about this in more detail. *Why* is it important to do this sometimes? *When* is the best time to do this? *How* can you make sure you fit this in? Talk about all your 'sometimes' and 'only if time' statements and think about *why*, *when* and *how*.

Now let's begin to plan. Let's suppose it is a typical school week. Planning your time carefully so that you can fit in all your priorities is called 'time management'. People who are good at managing their time usually feel less stressed by time. Is this an approach that might work for you? You wouldn't want to be doing it all the time, but would it be helpful when preparing for tests or when the school term first starts? Can you prepare lists ahead so that you remember to take things to school, etc? Can you use reminders such as Post-it notes or a calendar to help you remember important things? Talk to me about what you might gain from this approach. Let's draw up a plan for you on our own sheet of paper so that it looks a little like this. We can try it out this week and see if it helps your Worry Box stay quieter.

Weekly Timetable						
Time	**Activity**	**Monday**	**Tuesday**	**Wednesday**	**Thursday**	**Friday**

Session 12 — How did I do?

Look back at your timetable and see how you did.

Congratulations on all the work you have done on your Worry Box course. You now know a lot more about your Worry Box and how it affects you. Doing the course won't act like magic on your Worry Box, but you can now *choose* to use the approaches when you feel worried. Also, you should by now be better able to spot your Worry Box when it grumbles so that you know when to relax, think calm thoughts, find another way of dealing with things, or plan your time better.

Practise your approaches as you meet each stress and keep practising your relaxation and breathing. If you have been setting targets for your health or the way you deal with other people, then we might look at extending these so you can work for a larger goal and a bigger reward.

You need to know how proud we are that you have worked so hard on this and how pleased we are for you if you are beginning to feel better about things. Whenever you find that there is something worrying on your mind, write it on a piece of paper. Decide when the best time for worrying about it, and doing something about it, is going to be and then try to put it completely to one side until that time. You could put that piece of paper firmly into your work box and not get it out again until it is time to deal with it.

Worry list	
I am worried about . . .	**I will think about it when . . .**

Whenever your Worry Box starts to grumble, speak to it in your head 'NOW what are you worried about? What is your evidence that this will happen? That's nonsense because . . . so please be quiet and let me think!' Try to think of an example and practise.

This course means that you can now draw up a plan for managing your Worry Box so that you can control it more.

- **Spot** when your Worry Box starts to grumble. For example, what do you first notice? What is it for you?
- **Think** about what it is you can actually control and what you can't. For example, I can't stop the spelling test happening, but I can breathe slowly to reduce my heart rate and think more clearly.
- **Tell** yourself what to do. For example, 'Worry Box – be quiet – you are being silly and there is no evidence that I'm not clever. Leave me alone to think clearly!'
- **Action** – do it! For example, slow breaths, visit your special place, talk to someone, relax.

And now there's a special certificate for you. CONGRATULATIONS! Plan a treat to celebrate.

Worry Box Course

. . . .

has been working hard to control a noisy Worry Box
and has now come to the end of the course
Congratulations!

This is a REAL ACHIEVEMENT

Signed . . . .   Date . . . .

References

Mortimer, H. (2000) *Taking Part: Helping young children take part in a statutory assessment of their special educational needs*. Stafford: QEd Publications.

Mortimer, H. (2007) *Fireworks: Managing anger in young children*. Stafford: QEd Publications.

Useful books

Drost, J. (2004) *Bubblegum Guy: How to deal with how you feel*. Bristol: Lucky Duck Publishing (www.luckyduck.co.uk)

Hromek, R. (2005) *Game time: Games to Promote Social and Emotional Resilience for School Age Children*. London: Sage Publications (www.sagepub.co.uk)

Koeries, J., Marris, B. & Rae, T. (2004) *Problem Postcards: Social, Emotional and Behavioural Skills Training for Disaffected and Difficult Children aged 7–11*. London: Paul Chapman Publishing (www.paulchapmanpublishing.co.uk)

Mortimer, H. (2000) *Taking Part: Helping young children take part in a statutory assessment of their SEN*. Stafford: QEd Publications (www.qed.uk.com)

Mortimer, H. (2003) *Emotional Literacy and Mental Health in the Early Years*. Stafford: QEd Publications (www.qed.uk.com)

Mortimer, H. (2006) *Behaviour Management in the Early Years*. Stafford: QEd Publications (www.qed.uk.com)

Mosley, J. (1998) *More Quality Circle Time*. Cambridge: LDA (www.ldalearning.com)

Plummer, D. (2001) *Helping Children to Build Self-Esteem*. London: Jessica Kingsley Publishers (www.jkp.com)

Rae, T. (2001) *Strictly Stress: Effective Stress Management for High School Students*. Bristol: Lucky Duck Publishing (www.luckyduck.co.uk)

Sher, B. (1998) *Self-esteem Games*. Chichester: Wiley (www.wiley.co.uk)

Shotton, G. (2002) *The Feelings Diary*. Bristol: Lucky Duck Publishing (www.luckyduck.co.uk)

Useful resources

Being Yourself – hand puppets and therapeutic games for professionals working to improve mental well-being and emotional literacy in children (www.smallwood.co.uk)

Bridge of Self-Confidence – a therapeutic and educational game for helping coping skills (www.winslow-cat.com)